~Life's Diary~

Originally published in softcover
 by AuthorHouse, 2005

Revised edition, 2012

Printed in the United States of America

"We May Not Be On The Same Page But Were Definitely In The Same Book"

-LaChanda M. Gray

Table of Contents

To my family, who exhibits what "taking a village to raise a child" means, I appreciate the lessons that you all continue to teach me about life through the examples that you set...
I Love You All

♡

LIFE'S DIARY

I started to write the day you were born.
Throughout the years pages were torn
By Time's black hand that would arise;
Coming through to remind you of how it
flies.

You take me for granted
But to yourself be true.
When there are words to speak
And things to do

Just listen to what comes from me.
I'll shape your future mysteries.

There is so much to learn
And to see
Inside the book of
Life's Diary.

I AM

I am cool like
The winter winds
That blow.
I am the flower
That continues
To grow.

I am like the river
That flows so smooth
I am the cooking
Of soul food.

I am the money you spend
I am never a failure
I always win.

I am someone
Who will never
Let you down
Call on a friend
I am around.

NO SHAME

Are you soft as a sock
Or hard as a rock?
Are you smooth as silk
Or pour like fresh milk?

Do you walk
With your head held high
Or at the sight of trouble
run and cry?

Do you do your best with
Or without fame
I congratulate you
I see no shame.

JUST ME

Here I stand
With no aliases
But even if I did
I'd still be me.

No props
To control my victories
Just pen and paper
As words fall
From the sky
As you dissect me,
Pick at me,
The curious you
Asking why

But what answer
Can I give
To satisfy your needs?
When I give you the truth
Would your mind be pleased?

You haven't seen me
At my best
Haven't lived
Through my worst
Giving looks
When I pass
Asking no questions first.

I wish there was more
I could tell you
About the person
That you see
But the only thing I know
Is what I live for
And that's just being me.

CROOKED SONG

I sing of life
truth be told
determine what to tell
what to hold
making too much out of it
you got it all wrong
as you torture
disfigure my song.

Making too much
out of words
that are as plain as day
giving your opinion
to the life I live
by what I say.

Who are you
to judge,
criticize or characterize
my good and bad
my life is so simple not all that deep
do people try to read more into
what you say when you speak?

I'm the ordinary
that people seem to misjudge
because they don't have a clue

of how simple it is
when life haunts you

I'm living my life
so you got it all wrong
life is just what it is
so don't disfigure my song.

TRANSFORMATION OF LIFE

I'm not the girl
I use to be
learned to reflect
transformed into
another me.

Now, I know I don't
know it all
trying to be perfect
we tend to stumble and fall.

I'm a work of art,
apart of His masterpiece.
learning every day to
relax and release;

Instead of obsessing
over every day troubles
or running, hiding
with my head in a bubble.

Standing tall and strong
through whatever storms
may cross my path
to make me the rubble
of its aftermath.

Know your worth
without allowing others to change it
despite the scrapes and bruises
continue to claim it.

Within everything you say
and all that you do
make sure the life you live
is a reflection of you.

WHERE THE WIND BLOWS

Let life take you
where the wind blows.
Let it lead you
down the path of the unexpected;
to every tulip and every rose.

Let life take you
through every breeze;
to the lessons of love,
pain, and all life's mysteries.

Let life take you
through the storm.
Let it keep you safe
and keep you warm.

Through the bad and the good
and when you seem
to be misunderstood.

When you feel alone
and no one knows,
let life take you
where the wind blows.

Living everyday
as though it's your last
so that everyone in your future
can enjoy your past.

WHERE DID YOU COME FROM

Out of no where
You ventured into my sight
Leaving me speechless.
I became flattered
By your dazzling ways;
Touched by your kindness.
Cautious though
Never before have
I seen your type.
Where did you come from?

Even though we've just meet
Feels like I've known you a lifetime.
Never before have
I felt this way.
I'm overwhelmingly
Intrigued by your style,
Emotionally fulfilled
By your charm
And mentally uplifted
By your wit.
Who are you?
Where did you come from?

You are the kind of person
I can tell the world about
And even though
They've never met you

They'll smile in amazement.
You are who most girls
Dream about.
Pinch me,
I'm dreaming right?

You are the type
Girls have to sit back and wonder
Dang where did he come from?

I SAY THIS TO YOU

I say this to you because
I've heard it once before
Pinching of the heart
Knocking at the door.

It all seemed so real
But turned out not to be true
So this is what I ask
When I turn to you.

If you take my heart
Be careful
Don't let it brake
Throwing it around
As if it were fake.

It's real and fragile
Steadily growing everyday
So handle it with care
This is what I say.

LOVE

Love is pressure
Love is pain
Love is the sun
At times like the rain.

Love is like the wind
See how fast it goes
Love makes you think
You'll never really know.

Love can be rotten
And love can be sweet
Love can pick you up
Off of your feet.

Love is like a needle
It may hurt but will heal
Love is like a rose
It grows and peels.

Love can go like day
Or love can be dark as night
But when it's true love
Throughout its imperfections
Love is just right.

WHAT IS LOVE?

Love is the days
that I can hold you
in my arms.
Love is the days
when you keep me
safe and warm.

Love is when
you accept me
as your friend
and you show me that
your love
will never end.

Love is when trust
comes flowing through
and loving you isn't hard to do.

Love is when
you are always on my mind.
Love is a clear path
and not blind.

A clear path to a place
not seen;
love is the sunny days
the air smells so clean.

If love is so wonderful
I won't fight
or have a fit;
just tell me where it is
because I would love
to have it.

JUST ANOTHER NOTION

It's a different time
But the same place
Broken memories
I've tried to erase
A road once paved
My heart buried in
And now I'm here wondering
Why I'm doing this again.

We are linked like a chain
And I want to break free
If all it'll cause
Is heartache and misery.

There's no time
For games played
No time for promises broken
No time for treating love
As just another notion.

A GOOD MYSTERY

As I read your pages my heart
Unfolded to your story.
I became hooked from the start
As I set out to hear your glory.

I cried and prayed for you
That your happy ending
Would be fulfilled
My eyes closed tight,
In denial and without a clue
As my heart became your shield.

I thought your pages I had read
From beginning to the end
Imprinted inside my head
And cheering for you to win.

As I indulged my eyes
Into your soul
I discovered pages
Secretly left out
My heart broke
Turned cold
Because I discovered
What you were about

Now I know when I see a book
To compare it to another

I won't get caught up
In just the look
Choosing books with
Mysterious covers.

GIVING IN TO LOVE

You pretend to need me
You try to make me your all
Hoping and wishing
Into me you would fall.

At times you
Take me for granted
Like I owe you my time
You got it all twisted
All messed up
Because you're on my dime.

At times I forgive you
For the madness you show
But continue to do me wrong
To someone else I will go.

If your life
I fulfill do not mess it up
Because it could be your last
Make me your all and not times' past.

MY TREE

(To my grandparents)

You are my shade
When the sun is too bright.
You cool my path
While dimming the light.

You provide me a place
When I need to rest
An ear or shoulder
When I'm not at my best.

You reach out your arms
And open your heart.
You were there for me
From the start.

I am your leaves
And you are my tree
If there were no you
There would be no me.

IF YOU WERE NOT HERE

(To Deneasha, Jacque & Elizabeth)

I had a dream
that you were not here.
It brought me to my feet
brought me to tears.

If you were not here,
I don't know what I'd do;
maybe run a thousand miles
just to find you.

If you were not here,
I don't know what
anyone could say;
to patch up my heart
to make life okay.

If you were not here,
I don't know where I could go;
to continue to share the moments
we had long ago.

If you were not here,
I don't know who I could call;
to be as real as you
and give me their all.

This dream felt so real
and it continued for hours.
When I awoke I knew
I had to give you
your flowers.

To let you know
that I appreciate
all that you do,
and I'd be lost
if one day I didn't have you.

All the things I need to say;
one of my biggest fears
is not telling you I love you
if you were not here.

FOR YOU

I cry for you
When the sun is at rest
I wish I could
Take your burdens
And put them on my breast.

I cry for you
Before I cry for me
I ask God to ease your pains
And hear my plea.

When happiness
Seems to pass you by
I get on my knees and cry.

I sing for you
The songs of joy and hope
When things are just right
Or just a joke.

I sing for you
When it seems
To have taken your wind
I unlock my doors
And let your soul in.

When every road
Seems to sting
For you I sing.

I cry and sing
Like your story is my own
Because no one should face
The troubles of life alone.

I cry and sing
I pray for happiness
To come your way
Instead of your smile leaving
I pray it'll stay.

Through the love I feel
Through all of life's swings

For you
I pray
I cry
I sing.

THE MAN THAT SAW ME CRY

I poured my heart out
because I had troubles in the way.
As I cried he whispered to me and said,
"It'll be okay."

I shouted and screamed
with tears that flowed like a lake.
He gently brushed my cheek and said,
"Your grief I will take."

As I talked my word became chopped up
and in my head confusion ran.
He looked at me and said,
"My child take my hand."

The man that saw me cry
took my pain away.
The man that saw me cry
is in heaven and at night to him I will
pray.

WORDS NOT SPOKEN

Unsatisfied by life
Drowned by tears
Covered in truth
Turned into fears

Didn't know what to do
Or even what to say
Whenever we came your way

Life must have been dark
Out of control
Day by day playing
The same old role

A role of a man with
No beginning or end
The life where he
Had only one friend

But the love was still there
Buried deep down inside
The life with the bottle
That's where his love hides

But now his life is gone
And it's much too late
To work it out
To get it straight

The words he wanted
To say so long ago
To the ones he loved
But refused to show

Now further apart
Than a ride across town
It's all been put to rest
His soul not found

It all seem so clear
What use to be vague
He probably couldn't handle
The road that was paved

He went on living
Heart probably broken
From not saying the words
That was never spoken

WHEN SATAN IS AROUND

I thought I was cured
I thought I was free
Of all the pain
That would haunt me.

I try to walk in His steps
Try to make my life right
But it seems as though
I keep losing in Satan's fight.

Satan steadily tests me
Laughs at me
Spits at me
Pushes me down.

Likes to watch me
Fall on my face
Only then is when he knows
I bowed to his grace.

I'm running in circles
So how do I break away
From his craziness, madness,
I face day to day.

It's hard to be good
When you are treated bad.

Hard to be happy
When life gets sad.

Hard to make a way
When people put you down
Hard to be your best
When Satan is around.

INNER CONFRONTATION

I'm at war
My ship is slowly sinking
And I have no plan B
My ammunition is low and
My enemy is gaining on me.

Don't remember
When the war started
Too late to say
How I could have changed
The path that got me
To this day.

Can feel the pain
From the wound
That occurred on this path
From the rain, flood,
Hail and after math.

Can't see the sun
Can't seem to justify
Why the storm
Didn't pass me by.

Can't find my knees
Can't seem to pray
Even though that's why
I may be at war today.

He's right behind the door
And I want to keep it shut.
Don't know how long I can last
When my heart is in such a rut.

Outside I try to stay strong
But inside my strength is weak
On the inside my pain is strong
Although I try to avoid it
And stand on my feet.

I'm at war with myself
So how do I win
How do I break away
And get out of
The condition I'm in.

The quick sand is sinking
And I'm up to my neck in dirt
The snake is close to my heel
I'm afraid I might get hurt.

Don't want him
To take over my mind
And don't want to hurt again
So how should I choose
Whether I should lose or win?

LITTLE GIRL'S PRAYER

Oh help me!
I've cried all night long
My mother is on drugs
And my father is gone.

My friends have
Turned against me
And stabbed me in my back
You are my only friend
And that's a fact.

This world is messed up
All people do is sin
For money and power
Everyone tries to win.

Oh my God!
Hear me
And make this world see
That only with you
Is where they should be.

Dry my eyes
And take care
Of my fears
Forgive my lies
And catch my tears.

To me, you have been good
When things looked bad
You comforted my heart
When I was sad.

Oh God! Hear my prayer
And remember my name
So when I meet you in heaven
I'll have no shame.

While I strive to do your will
And make it my plan
To meet you in heaven my God
Amen.

CAN YOU FEEL ME?

Some people don't know
How much pain you can put
In people's lives
Just by one bullet or knife.

You can see so much pain
And pressure from the tears
Wanting others
To understand your fears.

But you don't seem
To understand who else you hurt
While a mother's child is buried
Six feet in the dirt.

You show no sympathy
For the ones in pain
If this was you
Would you react the same?

Just try to think twice
Before you pull the trigger
Pulling the trigger
Doesn't make you
A role model figure.

I hate the fact that people
Seek for revenge on another
Going after a
Sister, mother or brother.

What will it take
For you to see
The unnecessary bodies
That lay six feet deep
Can you feel me?

CAN YOU FEEL ME 2?

I silently sit
In my room thinking
Homes are left in silence
Shot before their time
Left alone to die
Can someone tell me why?

I hear gun shots
Explode in the air
Is there anyone out there
That cares?

As the person
Slowly passes away
Was it my friend/relative?
I can't say.

Dream that people
Put down their guns
Mothers and fathers
Be a role model
To daughters and sons.

Pray that people
Stop dealing and using drugs
Laughing as they
Classify themselves as
Role model thugs.

Pray for the ones
Without a place to stay
Hoping they'll live
To see another day.

For the ones
With nothing to eat
Ones with no shoes
On their feet.

When we learn
What He is trying
To make us see
Living in unity
This is how it should be
Once again
Can you feel me?

LIFE WITH NO PAUSE

The definition of life
is categorized by
the breath we take
but should it be?

As the clock continues to tick
you look up and ask
has this day really passed
or is it just me?

The assumption of life
has brought you back
like sentence that go on
with way too much slack.

Life is like a circle
that slowly closes
as it takes your wind.

Playing games
not even a kid
as you hold back
what's in your head
you think it's the beginning
when it might be the end.

You know it's not a game
mouth like fire
Heart of ice
watching you burn
in flames.

You say you've been blessed
but you sit there and complain
guess you think misery
only knows your name.

All because you thought
you saw a coma
you wait on something
that's not really there.

Start to talk like you
just got stuck with a knife
all because you didn't know
there's no pause after life.

LIFE WITH NO PAUSE 2

Life begins with an entrance not an end
Praying for a pain free life
I wouldn't recommend

If you want to place a period
Behind this sentence
I plead you beware
Of the darkness
That may follow
To the stroke of night
Be more like a game of hearts
Than red light green light.

Take heed to my warning
And consider my notion
Because life is like a train
That's been put into motion

When you're days into cries
That comes with a cause
Deal with it fast
Because life has no pause.

IF DEATH COULD TALK

If death could talk
What would it say?
Would it unleash the secrets
We hide from day to day?

If death could
Talk would it let us in
On all of life's secrets
Before taking our wind?

If death could talk
Would we be ashamed
To have set free
All the mistakes
We were too blind to see.

If death could talk
Would words comfort our souls
Or for the ones we love
Would it leave a big painful hole?

If death could talk
What would it have to say?
Ask yourself this question
As you plan out your day.

MY WORLD

When my girlfriend had our baby
it was the best day of my life.
I admit that I was scared
that things wouldn't go right.

I wanted to be with my daughter
be the best dad that I could be.
That was part of what I was thinking
when I asked my girlfriend to marry me.

She cried and cried so hard
I couldn't understand why
were those tears of sorrow
joy in her eyes.

She had cheated on me
but swore that my daughter was mine.
I was pissed how was I to know
if she was telling the truth
or just lying.

I loved my daughter so much
I couldn't live without her smile
but her mother made it hard for me mile
after mile.

Demanding more money,
on top of the money that I gave
she didn't care about nothing
but looking good and getting paid.

I could say I wish I'd never met her
but then there wouldn't be this little girl
who says I am her everything
and who is my world.

MY SISTA

My sista have you lost your mind?
He left you before
and now you're taking him back;
girlfriend you must be blind.

My sista are you crazy?
Trusting him with all your heart
after leaving you with a baby.

Girlfriend when will you learn?
That the man you thought you had
isn't only yours.

He's taking your money
and giving it to her to use;
while your bills are not paid
and you're stuck singing the blues.

Honey don't cry
I'm just telling you what's clever.
You are my sista and
I know you can do better.

You say that the advice
I'm giving you
is nothing you can use

This is your life and
only you can choose
My sista play smart.

TO BE OR NOT TO BE

I wasted no time deciding
to bring you into my home.
I felt that you were what I needed.
You would be the verdict of my life and I
would be the cause. I was overly eager to
have you invade my home and determine
my fate.
Now as you lay there in my sight I'm a bit
uneasy. You are here to tell me how I
should play out my life. You are here to let
me know whether my body is or is not
healthy. You are nothing but mean more
than life
Or rather not.

All this rushes through my head.
I look at you but decide
I can't go through with it.
I pick you up off the table
and put you in the closet.
I know you are out of my sight
But you're not off my mind.
This is crazy.
How bad could taking one test be?
I take the box out the closet.
Sit it on the table.
It took less than five minutes
to take the test.

Tick, tock, tick, tock...

A day for the results to come back.
Tick, tock, tick, tock
Status known
Do you know your status?
Be safe.
Protect yourself.

NEVER THOUGHT

I would not have thought
It would end like this
With the fire in your eyes
With the ball of your fist

Your emotions tempt to lead you
To a place unforeseen
I want to wake up quick
Feels like a bad dream

A person that I trusted
From years of my past
Has scared away my trust
Made it run fast

And because I know my worth
This is not what I need
I keep telling you no
As you beg and plead

Flashes of your actions
Stuck in my mind
Keep trying to move forward
But it's stuck on rewind

The meaning of love
That you tried to proclaim

It doesn't match up
Doesn't look the same

So through all the apologies
Promises and everything you say
Don't be surprised
As I continue to
Follow my trust
And walk the other way

TOO LATE

I feel in love a year ago
It was love at first sight.
On our first date he gave me roses;
Bought me dinner and gave me a small
kiss goodnight.

Oh my God cloud nine
Had nothing on me
I was treated like a queen
This had to be destiny.

Have you ever been so in love
That seeing your lover's face
Brought about an indescribable feeling?

Like you could fly but not fall
Palm sweaty. Heart beating fast.
Face carrying a smile.

Six months later
He asked me to be his bride.
I felt honored that someone
Would want to spend
The rest of their life with me
It filled an emptiness inside.

My parents disapproved
Said I didn't really know who he was.

I told them "I know all that I needed to
know, I know that I'm in love."

We got married immediately
there was no need to wait
No need to spend millions of dollars
or stress about the date.

The first day as Mrs. Right
I felt proud to be his wife
Couldn't tell you how many times
I dreamed about this life.

I made him breakfast in bed
To show him what a good woman he had
"Dang I burnt the bacon a little."
That pissed him off... made him mad.

I'd never seen him so angry
I apologized
it was my mistake
I ate the food I made
And fixed him another plate.

My husband loved me so much
He always wanted me by his side
And although I missed my family
I understood
I was his bride.

A secret trip to see my parents
Was twisted and turned upside down.
He thought that I was cheating
So he beat me to the ground.

Scared for six months straight
I couldn't move
Couldn't flee
Didn't know how to run
From the monster married to me.

I was finally set free
From the pain I had endured
The life I thought I wanted
But never really understood.

Ignoring the red flags
Cost me my life
And now someone else is his victim
Since I'm no longer his wife.

My parents come to visit me
Every now and then at my grave
They wondered where they went wrong
But they don't realize my life
Was only mine to save.

FINDING YOUR WAY

A blow to my face
Unleashed by my own hand
And without realizing
I continue again and again.

Keep losing apart of myself
As I carry unnecessary weight
Blind to my own demise
I'm unable to change my fate.

This is the struggle
That some of us face
As we continue to live our lives.
We load ourselves with luggage
And put on our best disguise.

We need to let go
Of the things that continue
To beat us down.
So let's grab a shovel dig
A grave and bury it
In the ground.

That's the only way
We can move forward
Break free from our inner fight
Move away from the darkness
And toward the inner light.

CONFUSION OF LIFE

Like a maze has twist
and turns so does life.
We weave ourselves in our webs
only to find ourselves
tangled in our own struggle.

We pack on layers
as though we are
lost in the cold.

We try to untangle the
deception and the misery.
Not knowing where our path
Starts or ends;
we feel defeated.

We give up on life.
On ourselves.

Oh! How confusion
can break us down.
Make us give up
on the greatest
value God
has given us.

Our mind is the poison.
To live is the cure.

CYCLE OF LIFE

Time seems to repeat itself
again and again ·
a targeted victim
of the violence
without a chance to win

I hold myself at fault
for the situations
I put into my life
I curse myself
become my battered wife

I stay true to hide
the tears inside
to avoid all the pain
from abuse and the sunny life
that's stained with the smell of rain

Would give my life
to change the destiny
of all the little people
after me that has been
targeted to feel my agony

I am only human
I can't blot out the stain
but I can talk you through life's rain

So you can grow up
to be a soldier, a lover
and not a battered wife
and you can tell someone else
how you defeated
the horrible cycle of life

RESCUE ME

I'm alone
In my room
But it's not quite.
Boom boom, boom
Boom boom, boom
Boom boom, boom.

Echoes the room
Mixed in with screams
Yells... flashbacks of pain.

I've been staring
At this white ceiling
A lot lately and it refuses
To bring me peace
It refuses to
Rescue me
It refuses to
Deliver me
From the noises
Filled between the walls.

Ugly, fat, stupid...
Black, white, gay...
Boom boom, boom
Boom boom, boom
Boom boom, boom.

Can't escape
These words
They follow me
Grades have hit
Rock bottom
Conduct is out
Of control

Unacceptable, inexcusable
Yells and screams
Boom boom, boom
Boom boom, boom
Boom boom, boom.
No one to turn to
So I turn to you
Rescue me
From this pain.

So I stare at the ceiling
Until you began to
Silence the screams
Unacceptable, inexcusable
Rescue me from
Ugly, fat, stupid…
Black, white, gay

Until you rescue me
From the
boom boom, boom
boom boom, boom
boom boom, boom.

FOR THEM

They try so hard
so that we can love them
but we continue
to push them aside.

As we go on
with the struggle
that child will never rise.

Why are we so big and bold
to push them off,
and fulfill a shattered heart?
Does the cut run so deep
that it destroys the life
we start?

Why does it take so long
to see the pain
we put them in?
Is it because
we are so selfish
we get caught up
in our own sins?

Who will cry
for them today?
Because no one has planned
for their tomorrow?

The rain pounding on their sheds
while they're feeding on their sorrows.
Who will stand
for them today?
Stand for those too small
to see in the crowd?

Who will do them justice?
Who will make them proud?

WHAT DO I DO?

I didn't know what I had done
that was so wrong in my life.
For them to keep coming at me
to try and pick a fight.

I wasn't taken serious
when I told my teacher
what they would do,
"Ignore them" I was told,
"they're just trying to scare you."

My parents are only concerned
with their jobs and straight A's.
Fusses at me when I don't focus
and don't understand my ways.

I get picked on in public
and many people pass us by.
Without a word or a hand
they just stare and watch me cry.

Who else is there to turn to
when I'm fighting on my own;
as they bully me around
and won't leave me alone.

What do I do
when no one will speak up
on my behalf?
When other kids just stare
or think it's funny,
funny enough to laugh.

What do I do when
I can't do any more?
No more than any other day?
When I'm given the impression
that no one cares
because they do nothing
but look the other way.

A NEW WORLD

Born with chains
The power to brake free
Didn't come to mind
As the poison was fed to me.

Going through life
Learning from day to night
But not realizing that left isn't left
If I call it right.

The trail of domination
That lay along my path
I shake my head
When I realize its aftermath.

To get to the truth
I have to brake free
Of the chains that
Continue to hold me.

I start with myself
Looking into the glass
Trickling down to a generation
Who don't care about the past.
Hard to pour on a transformation
When we're still filled
With a world that's content
With domination.

SYSTEM THAT REMAINS BROKE

One of the troubles of the world
is a system that remains broke.
Wealthy laughing at us down here
because they know it's a joke.

Can't make our ends meet
as they divide into four;
"The ones who has the most
Franklins can get many more."

This mentality that they live on
and in which too many die,
has many of us questioning
why, why, why?

"Because you're use to handouts
instead of making your own way."
That's what many people
have the audacity to say.

What about the people
who do what they can to stay on track,
but little to show for working hard all day
besides Peter and Paul on their backs.

When will we awaken
to see the trouble within our nation?
Instead of watching as it passes
from generation to generation.

We're so quick to draw a line
and choose a spot to stand;
but not quick enough
to put our heads together
and figure out a plan.

It's time to act now
instead of seeing it as just a joke.
If we don't it'll be a system
that remains broke.

A MONTH OF BLACK HISTORY?

"Why is there a month
dedicated to black people"

This is a question
I've been asked a lot lately

I've heard it
I've thought about it
and now to speak on it

Years ago our people
wore chains

Treated like dogs
as they slept out back

Treated like machines
as they worked all day
and when freedom came
still wasn't free

Through the years
whips were stained with blood

Bodies hung from trees
as if they were ornaments

and through the riots
and talks of change
cries were still being ignored

Still being treated
as an unworthy opponents

As years go by
you master your craft
Find other ways
to diminish our value

Like giving us a month to feel valuable
and then asking why we need it

A subtle slap in the face.
My friend this is the history
your ancestors have created for us

We were detached from the start

Our history will remain separate
as long as you continue to divide us

As long as you act as if the breath we take
is a favor given by you and as long as we
are put on a pedestal for a month
and none existent the days after

A month of black history?
Now a question like bells in my head

We don't need a month
We actually need at least twelve
to show the history
at least a decade
to show the survival
and a lifetime
to make you remember it.

UNLOCK THE DOOR

Our kids are struggling in school
and some have deemed them
destined to fail.

As if because of their class status
they'll either be nothing
or end up in jail.

Our kids are struggling in this world
without a stable place to stand.
Without anyone to step up
and offer out a hand.

Sometimes I think we
walk through life backwards
allowing us to slowly move ahead.
Instead of examining the problem
we'd rather be blind to them instead.

Unfortunately it's lead us to one thing
something we can't continue to ignore;
That it's hard to get to the progress
on the other side if we do nothing
but stare at a locked door.